W9-DET-811

COOL *STEAM* CAREERS

SMOKEJUMPER

WIL MARA

Published in the United States of America by Cherry Lake Publishing
Ann Arbor, Michigan
www.cherrylakepublishing.com

Content Adviser: Chuck Sheley, editor *Smokejumper* magazine, V.P. National Smokejumper Association
Reading Adviser: Marla Conn, ReadAbility, Inc.

Photo Credits: ©U.S. Department of Agriculture/http://www.flickr.com/CC-BY-2.0, cover, 1, 12, 19, 27; ©Lance
Cheung/U.S. Department of Agriculture/http://www.flickr.com/CC-BY-2.0, 5, 15, 20; ©Alaska Fire Service Photo, 6, 7, 8,
28; ©TFoxFoto/Shutterstock Images, 11; ©aorlemann/CanStockPhoto, 17; ©Mark Corbet, 18; ©Public Affairs Office
Fort Wainwright/http://www.flickr.com/CC-BY-2.0, 23; ©Forest Service Northern Region/http://www.flickr.com/
CC-BY-2.0, 24

Library of Congress Cataloging-in-Publication Data

Mara, Wil.
Smokejumper / Wil Mara.
    pages cm. — (Cool STEAM careers)
  "Readers will learn what it takes to succeed as a smokejumper. The book also explains the necessary educational steps,
  useful character traits, and daily job tasks related to the career in the framework of the STEAM (Science, Technology,
  Engineering, Art, and Math) movement. Photos, a glossary, and additional resources are included." Provided by
  publisher.
  Audience: Ages 8 – 12.
  Audience: Grade 4 to 6.
  Includes index.
  ISBN 978-1-63362-007-0 (hardcover) — ISBN 978-1-63362-046-9 (pbk.) — ISBN 978-1-63362-085-8 (pdf) —
  ISBN 978-1-63362-124-4 (ebook) 1. Smokejumpers—Juvenile literature. 2. Wildfire fighters—Juvenile literature. I. Title.

SD421.23.M364 2015
363.37'9—dc23   2014026593

Cherry Lake Publishing would like to acknowledge the work of
The Partnership for 21st Century Skills. Please visit *www.p21.org*
for more information.

Printed in the United States of America
Corporate Graphics

ABOUT THE AUTHOR

Wil Mara is an award-winning, best-selling author of more than 150 books, many of which
are educational titles for young readers. Further information about his work can be found at
www.wilmara.com.

TABLE OF CONTENTS

STEAM is the acronym for Science, Technology, Engineering, Arts, and Mathematics. In this book, you will read about how each of these study areas is connected to a career as a smokejumper.

TAKING FLIGHT TO WAGE THE FIGHT

Ty jogged up to his aunt's car after school. She was waiting in the parking lot reading a text message from her daughter, Liz. Ty slid into the front seat and buckled his seat belt. Aunt Jan put her phone away and started the car.

"Your cousin Liz is headed to fight a **wildfire**," said Aunt Jan. "She has to report to her base this afternoon. Thank goodness she is well trained and will have the help of other experienced smokejumpers."

Smokejumpers are often faced with fires like this.

Smokejumpers must be experienced with parachutes.

Ty shook his head. "Wow, that sounds like an exciting job, but also a little scary! I remember Liz telling me about her parachute training and years working as a firefighter."

Wildfires can be particularly devastating. During the **dry seasons** of the year, woodland areas lose much of their moisture, and the chances of a wildfire increase dramatically. And once a fire gets rolling, the wind becomes a major factor. The stronger it blows, the quicker the fire spreads. If the direction of the wind

Full gear is often worn during training.

Planes enable smokejumpers to reach fires that are otherwise inaccessible.

changes, the direction of the fire can also change. On average, there are about 75,000 wildfires per year in the United States, and these are responsible for the destruction of 5 million to 10 million **acres** (2 million to 4 million hectares) of woodland.

Once a wildfire gets going, it's a challenge to put it out. This is where the fascinating profession of smokejumping enters the picture. Put simply, a smokejumper is a firefighter who is sent to the scene of a fire by airplane. He or she usually arrives at the site using a parachute. Smokejumpers have been around since the 1930s and are most common in the United States and Russia. In the United States, women have been a part of the smokejumpers since 1982 and in Russia since 1936. The first smokejump in the **suppression** of a wildfire occurred in 1940 in the Nez Perce National Forest in Idaho.

In the United States, smokejumping is more common in the western states because there is more undeveloped land there than in the East.

THINK ABOUT SCIENCE

Smokejumping is a part of firefighting, and the proper way to fight a fire is a science in itself. Fire is defined as a state of **combustion**, a chemical process that produces heat and light in flammable material. The best smokejumpers are those who understand how fire works—and how best to shut it down— through careful study of the science involved.

Only the Best

The idea of zooming through the air in a plane and then jumping out of it in order to help fight a forest fire sounds pretty exciting, doesn't it? As with any other profession, smokejumping requires a specific set of skills and talents.

Believe it or not, the most important experience you need for a job in smokejumping isn't parachuting. It's **wildland** firefighting. Think about it—parachuting is simply the way to get to the fire. If you don't know what to do *after* you get there, you're going to have serious problems. To qualify for the federal smokejumper

You must be a trained and experienced wildland firefighter before you can be a smokejumper.

Hotshot crews work in rough and remote areas.

training program in the United States, you should have either a bachelor's degree in a related field such as forestry or range management, at least five seasons of firefighting experience in these fields, or some combination of education and experience. Many newly hired smokejumpers have experience on a hotshot crew. Hotshots are **elite** teams of wildland firefighters.

Like any other job, smokejumping is not for everyone. A smokejumper may have to parachute into an affected area with one other jumper and determine the best course of action. But at the same time, the smokejumper will be working with other firefighters (both those in the air and those arriving by vehicles) in a group effort. Another important personal trait is the ability to adapt to rapidly changing situations. Remember that no two wildfires are alike and that the weather—being as unpredictable as it is—can alter a fire in a matter of seconds. The best smokejumpers are those who have what's known as a can-do attitude. The fire will work

THINK ABOUT ART

No two wildfires are alike, and a smokejumper must make split-second decisions about how best to approach every blaze. This often requires inventive thinking, where all the available facts have to be gathered together and then considered in a way that is wholly original. It's like art, which is all about creativity, but it's a challenging art form for sure!

aggressively to move forward, so the smokejumper has to work aggressively to bring it to a halt.

Finally, the ideal **applicant** for a smokejumper position is someone in excellent shape. The job is physically demanding. It is not unusual, for example, for a smokejumper to be at the site of a fire for 12 hours or more. Smokejumpers also need to carry equipment with them, sometimes over long stretches of land.

Working long hours under harsh conditions is typical for a smokejumper.

CHAPTER 3

ON THE JOB

The life of a smokejumper can be very exciting and rewarding. A smokejumper's job is certainly not like a typical office job. You will not be spending much time sitting behind a desk or in front of a computer. The hours will be unpredictable since a fire can start at any moment. So if you're looking for a comfortable routine, don't become a smokejumper!

Once that call comes in, you need to report immediately to your local base. This is where your equipment will be waiting, along with the plane that will take you to the site of the blaze. You will need to wear a jumpsuit built to protect you from trees and rocks on your landing. You'll also wear boots, a helmet with a protective mask attached, and gloves. You'll likely have to bring along many basic survival tools, such as a flashlight, knife, compass, first-aid kit, cell phone, radio, and weather instruments.

A drip torch like this is used by professionals to set fires in specific areas.

Tools like these Pulaskis are used often when fighting fires.

Equipment specific to firefighting can include a **drip torch**, shovel, and other hand tools like an ax, and even a chainsaw. The Pulaski, a hand tool with an ax blade on one end and a **trenching** tool on the other, is the tool used most often among smokejumpers. A smokejumper also brings along a small tentlike shelter called a fire shelter. Food and water will be required, although it has to be very light and compact. And, of course, you'll use a parachute.

Once in the air, you will be flown to the location of

the blaze. Then you'll jump from the plane and steer your parachute down to a safe area not far from the fire. You must quickly judge the situation and send information to your co-workers in the sky. The details you provide will help create a plan to fight the fire.

There are two approaches to wildfire suppression. Direct attacks are used to snuff out the blaze at its

Smokejumpers need to look for a safe place to land, not too far from the fire, but not too close either.

Smokejumpers watch closely to see how a fire moves and behaves.

source. Indirect attacks contain the fire and then let it burn out on its own. You may have to determine the best places to create a fire line—an area where there is no vegetation—so that the fire will die out when it reaches that point. Ninety percent of the time, a fire line will have to be created. Fire lines don't often occur naturally. You'll also have to estimate the best spots for firefighters in the air to drop fire-**retardant** chemicals so they'll have the greatest impact on the blaze.

A smokejumper's job isn't done once the blaze is no

longer a threat. Many jumpers also take part in the postfire "mop-up" effort. It's important to note that a fire that has been put out can always get going again. **Embers** can reignite at any time, especially during a dry season or when it's particularly windy. One single ember permitted to float away can land in another part of the forest and start the cycle all over again. There are numerous ways of cooling the burn area so as to smother all remaining threats. Only then is the smokejumper's job complete.

THINK ABOUT MATH

Mathematics figures heavily into the smokejumper's job. Calculating the precise location in which to parachute requires some mathematical thinking, as does estimating the quantity of fire-retardant material that may be needed to smother a blaze. This is one part of the job where the numbers need to be just right, because mistakes can be very costly.

Risk and Reward

By now you may be thinking that being a smokejumper could mean being at risk for certain dangers. No matter how many precautions you take, it is impossible to absolutely guarantee one's safety. A smokejumper's parachute is packed by a Federal Aviation Administration parachute rigger. A rigger is someone who is trained to pack and maintain parachutes. There have been no smokejumper deaths related to an improperly packed parachute.

This Alaska smokejumper is checking a parachute.

One of the greatest rewards of smokejumping is knowing you are helping to save wildlife.

Once you're on the ground, you have to be mindful of where the fire is, and—perhaps more importantly— where it's going. A wildfire can change direction quickly, and on a very dry day it can speed across the land. Another risk, more common than you might imagine, is falling trees. Trees that have already died, or are nearly dead, but are still standing are particularly dangerous.

In addition to the risks, there are certainly rewards involved with being a smokejumper. Smokejumpers experience great satisfaction knowing they are taking part in an effort to keep a fire from burning out of control. They are also credited with saving acres of unspoiled wilderness and everything that lives there.

Most of the time, the job is performed outdoors. This could be, for some, more appealing than working in an office or a factory all day. Smokejumpers get to enjoy the advantages of working both independently and as part a team.

THINK ABOUT ENGINEERING

An engineer, by definition, uses scientific knowledge to create practical applications. A smokejumper analyzes all aspects of fighting a fire to do the best job possible. He or she uses available equipment in a way that succeeds in putting out fires.

TODAY AND TOMORROW

In the United States the majority of work in this field is found in the northwestern part of the United States—Oregon, Washington, Idaho, and Montana. This is mostly because these areas have the largest stretches of undeveloped wildland in the country and are therefore more susceptible to fire outbreaks. There are also smokejumpers based in Redding, California, and in Fairbanks, Alaska. The first smokejumper bases were established in Missoula, Montana, and Winthrop, Washington, in 1940.

Smokejumpers are busiest during the warmer months, when forests are driest and most **vulnerable** to blazes. This is often called the fire season and usually stretches from late spring to early fall. In Alaska, fire season starts in April. In California the season can last into November. The rest of the year, smokejumpers may

The mission of smokejumpers from this fire center in Boise, Idaho, is to be the first on the scene when fires occur in remote areas.

These smokejumpers are reviewing a video taken by a camera mounted on a smokejumper's helmet.

have to find other employment on their own or be given other assignments to keep them active.

Some firefighter positions are considered volunteer jobs and are therefore nonpaying. But all smokejumpers earn a paycheck—none are volunteers. Median salary is around $35,000. The median salary is the wage that half the workers earn more than and half earn less than. This number can be much higher depending on your location and your work experience.

The growth rate for smokejumping positions is less than that of other professions, only about 3 or 4 percent annually. However, people do leave to take other positions all the time, sometimes remaining as firefighters but with different assignments. So there are still opportunities. Similarly, anyone interested in becoming a smokejumper might want to consider pursuing a more typical firefighting position first since firefighter experience is required for a smokejumper's job.

THINK ABOUT TECHNOLOGY

Firefighting technology is changing and improving all the time. Each technological advancement provides a better way to fight fires. In smokejumping, as in any other profession, it is critical that you keep up on all of the latest technological developments, in everything from equipment to training methods. One small detail could make the difference between success and failure.

THINK ABOUT IT

After reading this book, are you able to explain to a friend how a smokejumper works alone and as part of a group?

Visit the library or go online to find more information about becoming a smokejumper. How is the information similar to or different from the information you've read in this book?

Read chapter 3 again. A good understanding of mathematics is important for smokejumpers. For example, smokejumpers may need to know wind speed. Are you able to come up with three reasons why this piece of information is important?

LEARN MORE

FURTHER READING

Gigliotti, Jim. *Smoke Jumpers*. North Mankato, MN: The Child's World, 2014.

Goldish, Meish. *Smokejumpers*. New York: Bearport Publishing, 2014.

Gordon, Nick. *Smoke Jumper*. Danbury, CT: Scholastic Library, 2012.

Hubble, Robert D. *Limey Smokejumper: Fighting Wildfire in the Rockies*. CreateSpace, 2013.

WEB SITES

Spotfire Images—Wildfire Photojournal
www.spotfireimages.com
View thousands of dramatic smokejumping photos on this site.

Wonderopolis—What Is a Smokejumper?
http://wonderopolis.org/wonder/what-is-a-smokejumper
Watch a video and learn more about the details of how smokejumpers prepare for and do their jobs.

GLOSSARY

acres (AY-kurz) areas of land that measure a total of 43,560 square feet each; an acre is almost the size of a football field

applicant (AP-li-kuhnt) someone who applies for something, such as a job

combustion (kuhm-BUS-chuhn) the moment when a flame appears, starting a fire

drip torch (DRIP TORCH) a fuel-filled container used to start a fire in a designated area

dry seasons (DRYE SEE-zuhnz) times of year when forests are driest and fire is most likely to occur

elite (i-LEET) the best of a class of people

embers (EM-burz) materials that are still burning but do not have a flame

retardant (ri-TAHR-duhnt) resistant to flame

suppression (suh-PRESH-uhn) act of putting out a fire

trenching (TREN-ching) able to cut a long, narrow channel in the earth

vulnerable (VUHL-nur-uh-buhl) in a position or condition where a person or thing could easily be damaged

wildfire (WILDE-FYR) a large-scale fire that occurs in a forested area

wildland (WILDE-land) land that has not been cultivated, especially land set aside and protected as a wilderness

INDEX

[21ST CENTURY SKILLS LIBRARY]

AR Level ___6___ Lexile _1000_

AR Pts. _0.5_ RC Pts._____